1 2 3 4 5 2

Jenny Ackland

# Fun with Numbers

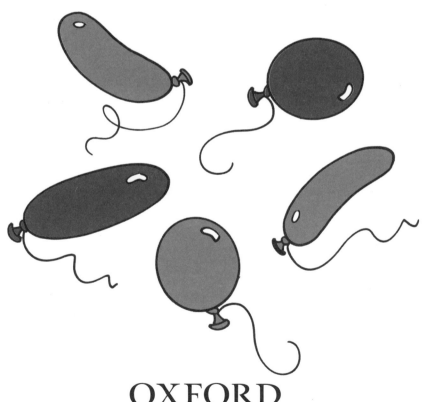

OXFORD
UNIVERSITY PRESS

1 2 3 4 5 1 2

# Introduction

These workbooks introduce and reinforce basic numeracy and literacy concepts for pre-school and Reception Year children. They give children opportunities to develop and to practise some of the skills that are assessed in the Foundation Stage Profile, which is completed before children move into Year 1. The activities should be fun and are designed to stimulate discussion as well as practical skills. Some children will be able to complete activities alone, after initial discussion; others may benefit from adult support throughout.

*Fun with Numbers* offers a variety of activities which focus, in particular, on the following skills:

- hand–eye co-ordination
- recognition, understanding and writing of numbers 1 to 5
- counting and sequencing up to 5
- identifying sets of particular quantities
- understanding the terms 'more' and 'less'
- basic addition and subtraction.

Oxford University Press
Great Clarendon Street, Oxford OX2 6DP

Oxford University Press is a department of the University of Oxford.
It furthers the University's objective of excellence in research, scholarship, and education by publishing worldwide in
Oxford  New York  Auckland  Cape Town  Dar es Salaam  Hong Kong  Karachi
Kuala Lumpur  Madrid  Melbourne  Mexico City  Nairobi  New Delhi
Shanghai  Taipei  Toronto

With offices in
Argentina  Austria  Brazil  Chile  Czech Republic  France  Greece  Guatemala
Hungary  Italy  Japan  Poland  Portugal  Singapore  South Korea  Switzerland
Thailand  Turkey  Ukraine  Vietnam

Oxford is a registered trade mark of ©Oxford University Press
in the UK and in certain other countries

© Jenny Ackland 2005
The moral rights of the author have been asserted
Database right Oxford University Press (maker)
First published 2005

British Library Cataloguing in Publication Data
Data available

ISBN-10: 0-19-838438-6
ISBN-13: 978-0-19-838438-0

Pack of 6
ISBN-10: 0-19-838436-X
ISBN-13: 978-0-19-838436-6

Pack of 36
ISBN-10: 0-19-838437-8
ISBN-13: 978-0-19-838437-3

1 3 5 7 9 10 8 6 4 2

Designed by Red Face Design
Illustrations by Mark Brierley, Oxford Illustrators
Printed in China

# Contents

# Number 1

Write number 1.

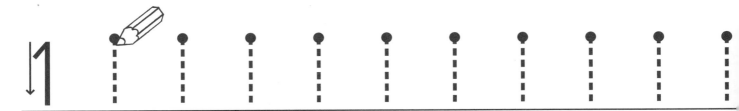

Give each dog 1 spot.

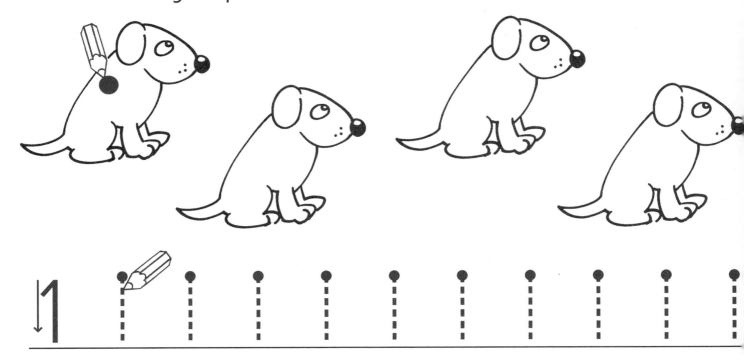

Give each cat 1 spot.

# Recognizing 1

Colour 1 balloon.

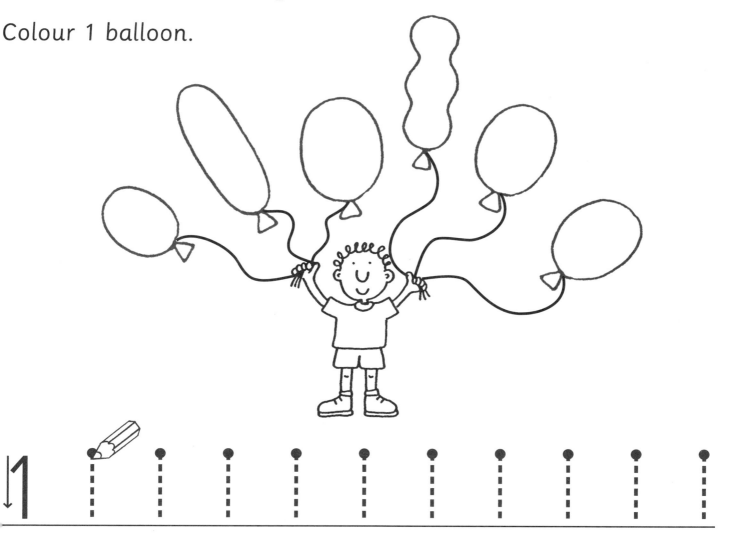

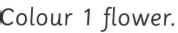

Colour 1 flower.

# Number 2

Write number 2.

Give each ladybird 2 spots.
Colour the ladybirds.

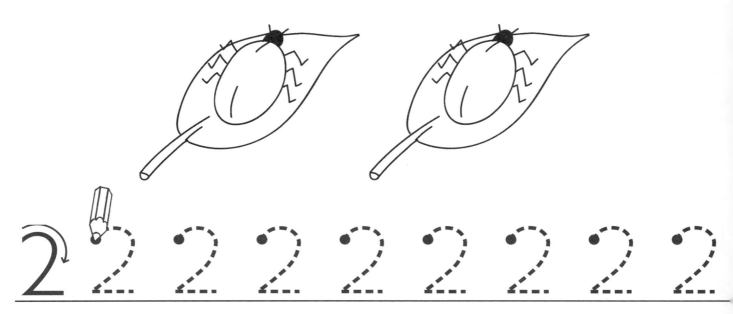

Give each butterfly 2 spots.
Colour the butterflies.

# Recognizing 2

Colour 2 fish.

2 2 2 2 2 2 2 2 2

Colour 2 cars.

# Sets of 1

Ring the trees with 1 apple.

# Sets of 2

Ring and colour the sets of 2.

# Sets of 1 and 2

Ring and colour the sets of 1.
Join them to the number 1.

Ring and colour the sets of 2.
Join them to the number 2.

# Counting 1 or 2

Write over the numbers.

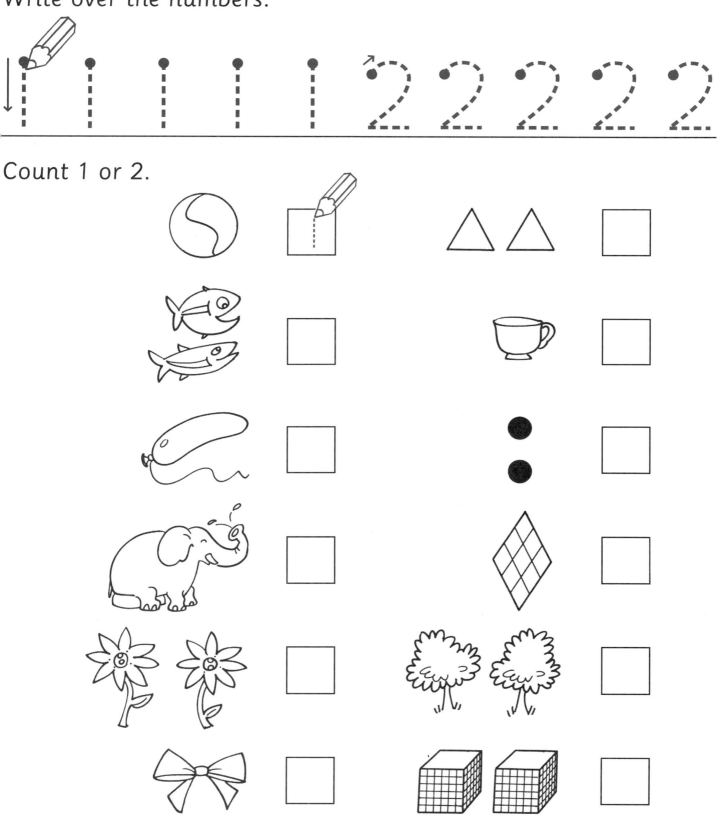

Count 1 or 2.

# Number 3

Write number 3.

Give the balloon 3 spots.
Colour 3 trees.

# Sets of 3

Ring and colour the sets of 3.

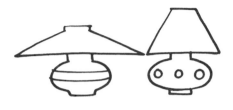

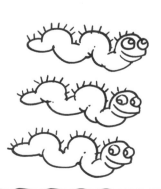

# Counting 1, 2, 3

Write over the numbers.

1 | | | | | | | | | | |

2 2 2 2 2 2 2 2 2 2 2

3 3 3 3 3 3 3 3 3 3 3

How many?

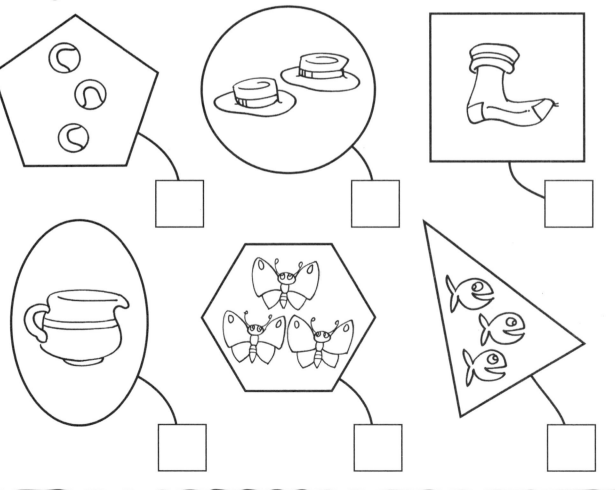

# Counting 1, 2, 3

Write over the numbers.

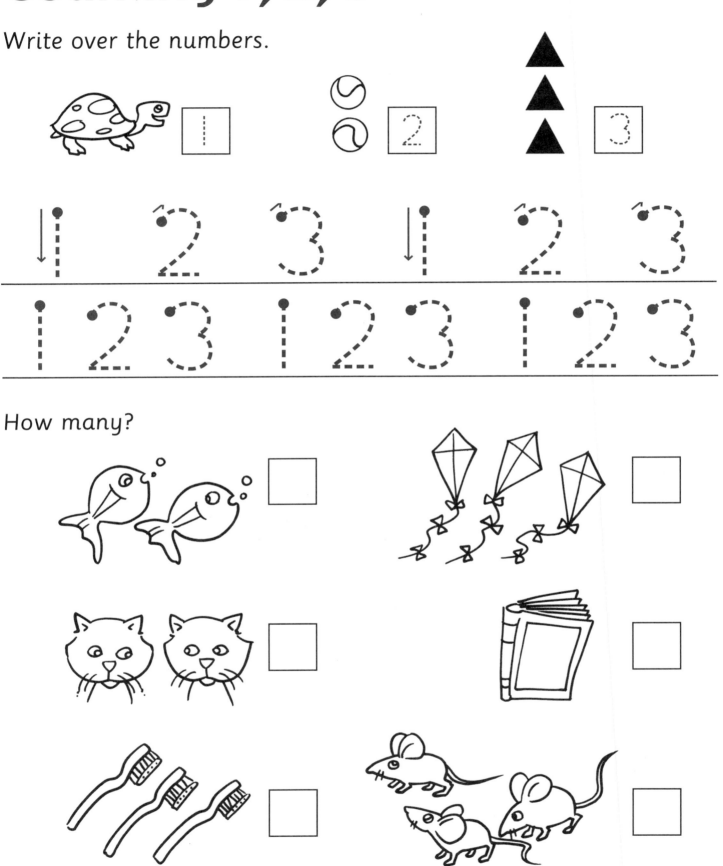

How many?

# Number 4

Write number 4.

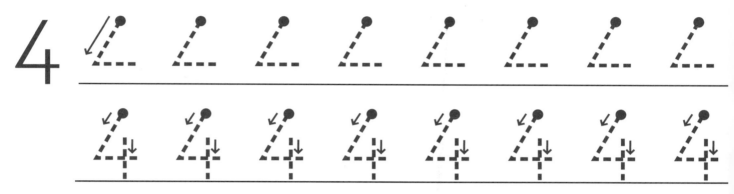

Colour 4 fish in each picture.

# Sets of 4

Ring and colour the sets of 4.

# Using 3 and 4

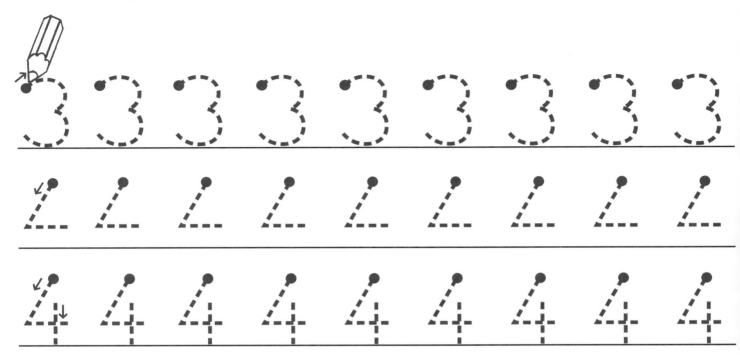

Read the numbers, then give the bugs 3 or 4 spots.

# Counting 1, 2, 3, 4

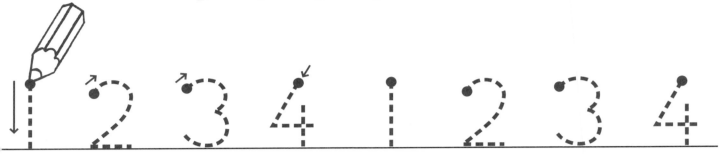

Count the pictures, then colour them.

# Number 5

↓⌐5  ˙ᒥ  ᒥ  ᒥ  ᒥ  ᒥ  ᒥ  ᒥ  ᒥ  ᒥ

↓5  ↓→2  5  5  5  5  5  5  5  5

Colour 5 hats.

# Sets of 5

Ring and colour the sets of 5.

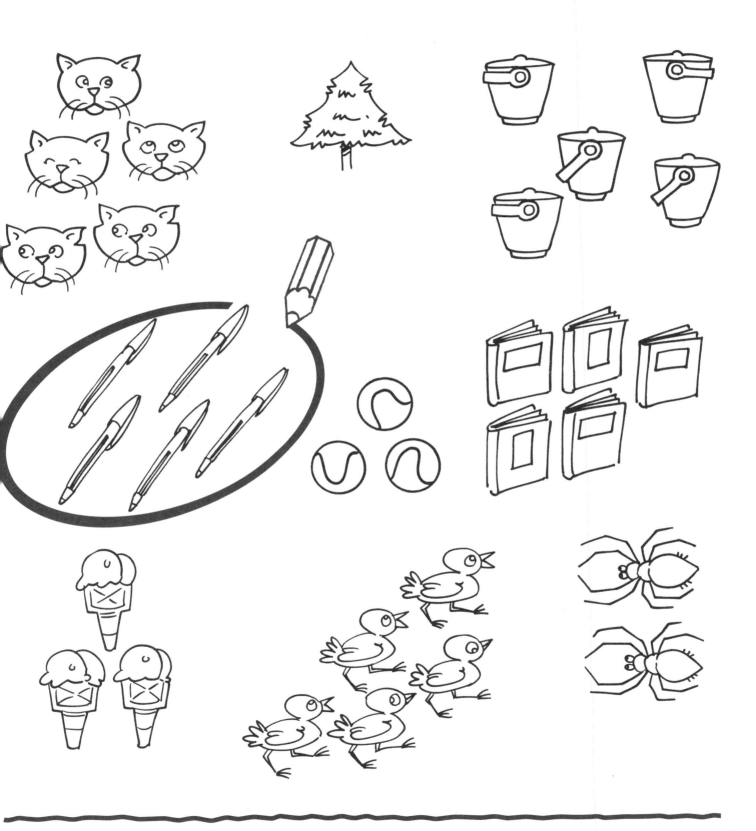

# Counting 1, 2, 3, 4, 5

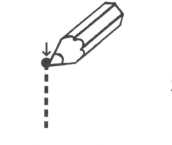   

*Colour the pictures.*

1   fish

2   rabbits

3   flowers

4   balls

5   trees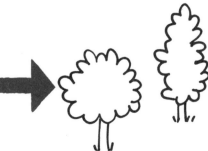

# Counting 1, 2, 3, 4, 5

Count the pictures and circle the number.

 (1) 2 3 boot

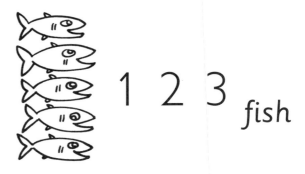 1 2 3 fish

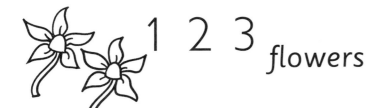 1 2 3 flowers

1 2 3 balloon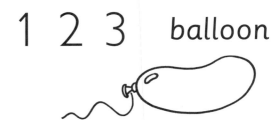

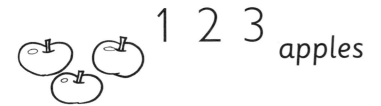 1 2 3 apples

 1 2 3 house

 1 2 3 rabbits

 1 2 3 balls

# How many?

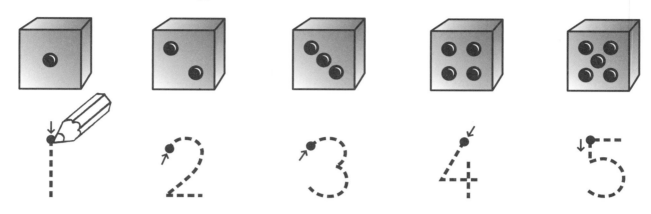

Give the snakes their spots.

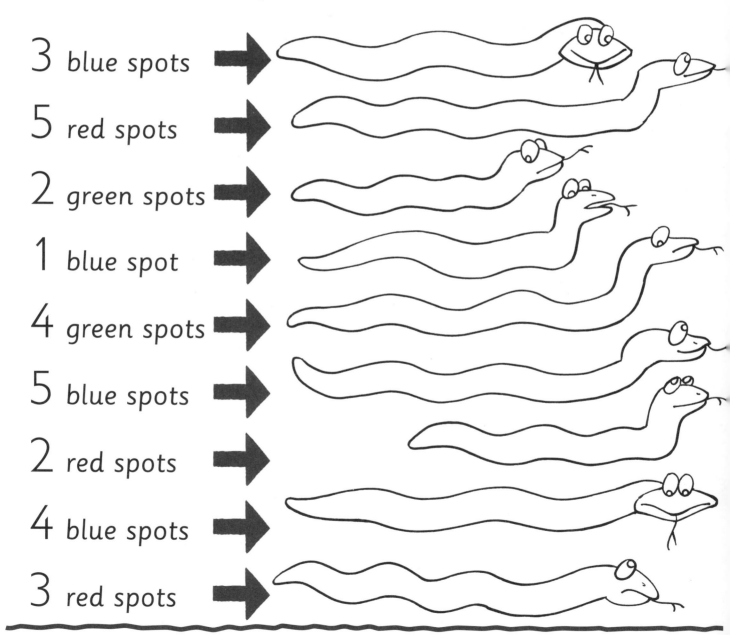

3 blue spots ➡

5 red spots ➡

2 green spots ➡

1 blue spot ➡

4 green spots ➡

5 blue spots ➡

2 red spots ➡

4 blue spots ➡

3 red spots ➡

# How many?

1 2 3 4 5

## How many spots?

# More or less?

Which set has more fish? Ring and colour it.

# More or less?

Which set has less hats? Ring and colour it.

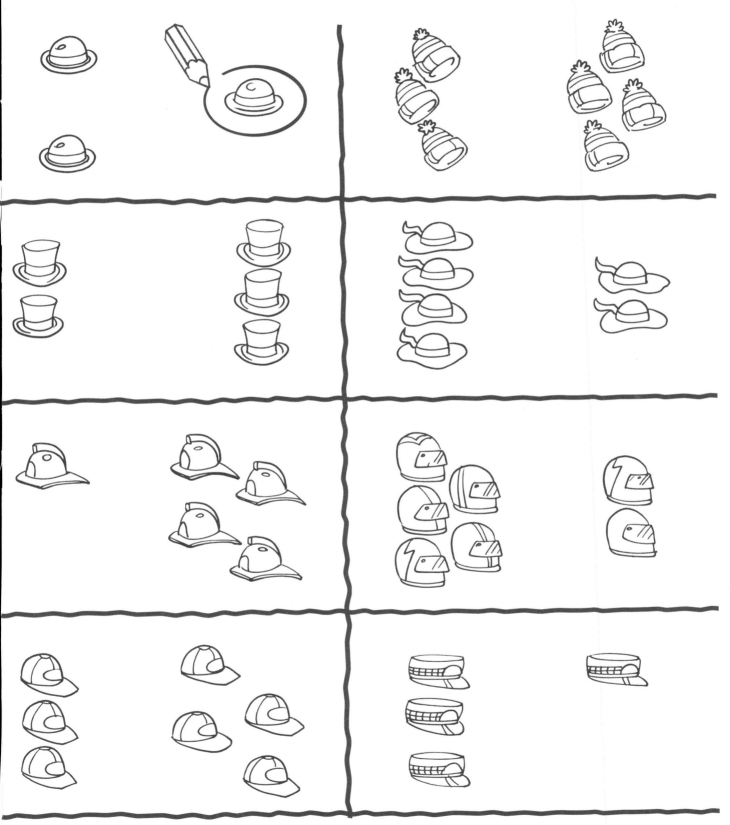

# Adding 1

0     1     2     3     4     5

Add 1 more spot to each animal.
Count the spots on each animal.

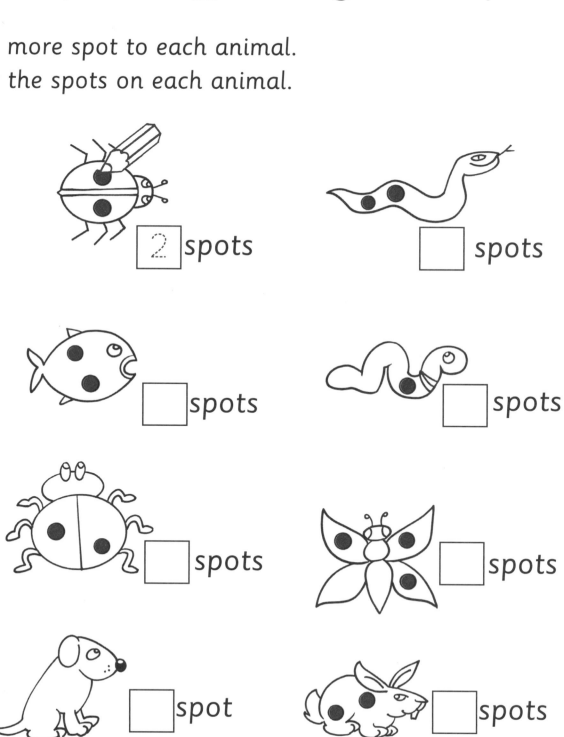

2 spots     ☐ spots

☐ spots     ☐ spots

☐ spots     ☐ spots

☐ spot

☐ spots

# Adding 2

Add 2 more legs to each animal.
Count the legs on each animal.

Now there are ☐ legs.

Now there are ☐ legs.

Now there are ☐ legs.

Now there are ☐ legs.

Now there are ☐ legs.

Now there are ☐ legs.

# Take 1 away

Take away the last number in each row.
How many are left?

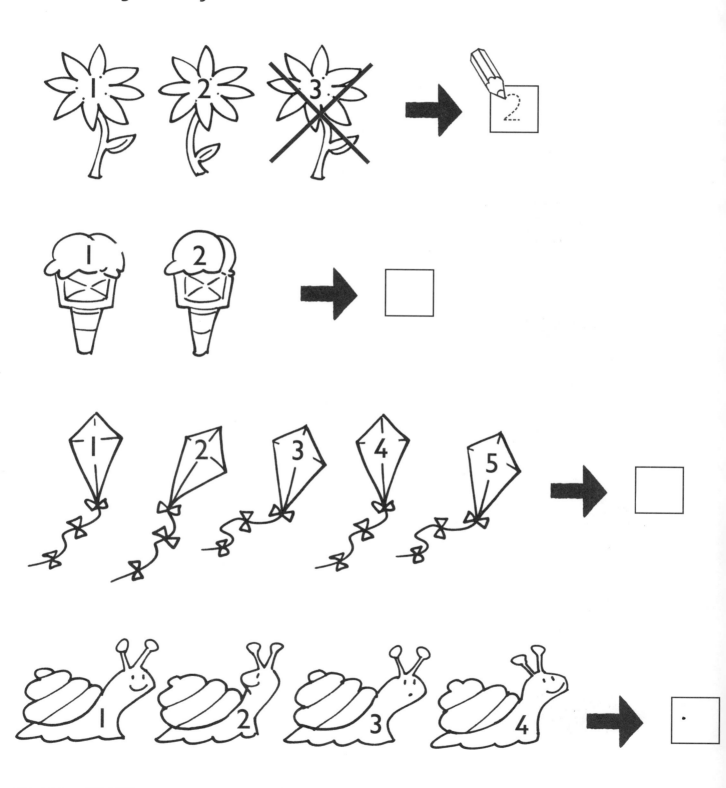

# Take 2 away

Take away the last 2 numbers in each row.
How many are left?

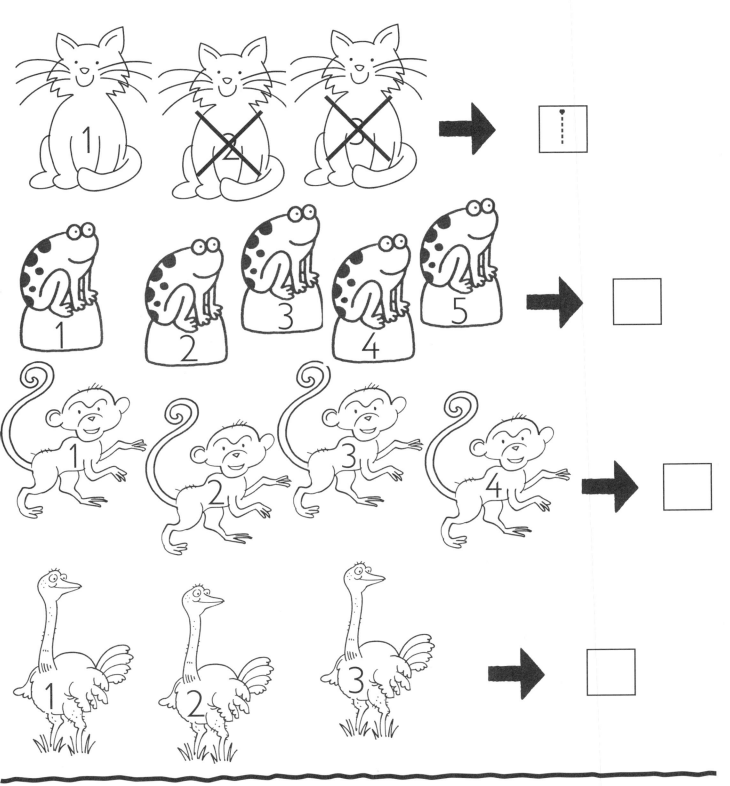

# Summary of skills

**Fun With Shape and Size**

Pack of 6
ISBN-10: 0-19-838433-5

ISBN-13: 978-0-19-838433-5

Pack of 36
ISBN-10: 0-19-838434-3
ISBN-13: 978-0-19-838434-2

**Fun With Reading**

Pack of 6
ISBN-10: 0-19-838424-6

ISBN-13: 978-0-19-838424-3

Pack of 36
ISBN-10: 0-19-838425-4
ISBN-13: 978-0-19-838425-0

**Fun With Writing**

Pack of 6
ISBN-10: 0-19-838427-0

ISBN-13: 978-0-19-838427-4

Pack of 36
ISBN-10: 0-19-838428-9
ISBN-13: 978-0-19-838428-1

**Fun With Counting**

Pack of 6
ISBN-10: 0-19-838430-0

ISBN-13: 978-0-19-838430-4

Pack of 36
ISBN-10: 0-19-838431-9
ISBN-13: 978-0-19-838431-1

**Fun With Numbers**

**Pack of 6
ISBN-10: 0-19-838436-X**

ISBN-13: 978-0-19-838436-6

Pack of 36
ISBN-10: 0-19-838437-8
ISBN-13: 978-0-19-838437-3